SPOTLIGHT
ON CHILDREN'S
AUTHORS

SHEL SILVERSTEIN

JOHANNAH HANEY

Cavendish
Square

New York

Published in 2014 by Cavendish Square Publishing, LLC
303 Park Avenue South, Suite 1247, New York, NY 10010
Copyright © 2014 by Cavendish Square Publishing, LLC
First Edition

This publication represents the opinions and views of the author based on his or her personal experience, knowledge, and
research. The information in this book serves as a general guide only. The author and publisher have used their best
efforts in preparing this book and disclaim liability rising directly or indirectly from the use and application of this book.

CPSIA Compliance Information: Batch #WW14CSQ
All websites were available and accurate when this book was sent to press.

Library of Congress Cataloging-in-Publication Data
Haney, Johannah.
Shel Silverstein / Johannah Haney.
pages cm. — (Spotlight on children's authors)
Includes bibliographical references and index.
ISBN 978-1-62712-271-9 (hardcover) ISBN 978-1-62712-272-6 (paperback) ISBN 978-1-62712-273-3 (ebook)
1. Silverstein, Shel—Juvenile literature. 2. Authors, American—20th century—Biography—Juvenile literature. 3.
Illustrators—United States—Biography—Juvenile literature. 4. Children's literature—Authorship—Juvenile literature. I.
Title.

PS3569.I47224Z68 2014
818'.5409—dc23
[B]

2013030185

Editorial Director: Dean Miller
Senior Editor: Peter Mavrikis
Copy Editor: Cynthia Roby
Art Director: Jeffrey Talbot
Designer: Amy Greenan
Production Manager: Jennifer Ryder-Talbot
Production Editor: Andrew Coddington
Photo research by Julie Alissi, J8 Media

The photographs in this book are used by permission and through the courtesy of: Cover photo by Alice Ochs/
Contributor/Michael Ochs Archive/Getty Images; Everett Collection/Newscom, 4; Chicago History Museum/Contributor/
Archive Photos/Getty Images, 6; John Sones Singing Bowl Media/Lonely Planet Images/Getty Images, 8; SuperStock/
SuperStock/Getty Images, 10; Henri Silberman/Workbook Stock/Getty Images, 12; Piero Oliosi/Polaris/Newscom, 14; ©
Sports Illustrated, 14; John Picken/ Chicago skyline from 16th Street bridge/Flickr/Creative Commons Attribution 2.0
Generic license, 16; Anton Zelenov/ St. Basil Cathedral/Creative Commons Attribution–Share Alike 3.0 Unported license,
19; Photo by Volanthevist/Flickr/Getty Images, 19; Jan Cobb Photography Ltd/Photographer's Choice/Getty Images, 19;
S.Borisov/Shutterstock.com, 19; Digital Vision./Digital Vision/Getty Images, 20; © iStockphoto.com/AngiePhotos, 27;
Gems/Contributor/Redferns/Getty Images, 28; © AP Images, 30; ableimages / Alamy, 32; Alice Ochs/Contributor/Michael
Ochs Archives/Getty Images, 34; Alice Ochs/Contributor/Michael Ochs Archives/Getty Images, 37.

Printed in the United States of America

CONTENTS

INTRODUCTION

When Shel Silverstein returned home from serving in Japan in the military, he felt lost. He had just spent two years writing cartoons full-time for a military newspaper. But now he had no job, no plans, and was living with his parents. Shel wandered the streets of his native Chicago, dropping off samples of his cartoons to any magazine editors who would look at them. Shel's work life, however, did not remain bleak for long.

Soon, Shel started selling his cartoons. His friend, children's author Tomi Ungerer, urged him to write for children. He reluctantly agreed to try. Shel's friend Ron Haffkine describes watching Shel write his children's stories and poems: "As he worked, he hunched over his desk, his long bony fingers drew and redrew each character and he giggled to himself like a child. There would be quiet for a while, then a burst of laughter. It was as though he were enjoying something that someone else had created especially for him."

Shel wrote all the time. He rarely went anywhere without a pad of paper and a pen. If he had an idea and no paper, he was known to write on anything available to him. Lisa Rogak, Shel's biographer, writes, "He'd start in on the napkins at a fancy restaurant, then move on to the tablecloth. When he had that completely covered, or if he was walking down the street, he'd start doodling on his hands, his shirtsleeves."

Although he made friends with many famous actors, writers, and musicians, fame was never important to Shel. Fortune did not motivate him either. His publishers used to remind him to cash his checks because they were sometimes so big that leaving them uncashed would cause a huge imbalance in the company's accounting system.

More than 29 million copies of his books for children have been sold to date, and they have been translated into more than 30 languages.

Shel Silverstein was born in Chicago during the Great Depression.

Chapter 1
EARLY LIFE

"I would hope that people, no matter what age, would find something to identify with in my books, pick one up and experience a personal sense of discovery."
(Publisher's Weekly *interview*)

On September 25, 1930, a baby boy named **Sheldon Allan Silverstein** was born in Chicago, Illinois. His mother was named Helen and his father was Nathan. They called their son Shel.

Shel's father immigrated to the United States fifteen years before Shel was born and started a bakery with his brother Jack called Silverstein Brothers Bakery. In the 1930s in the United States, many people were struggling financially. The Great Depression gripped the nation, making it difficult for families to find enough money for food and other basics. Shel's father brought home day-old bread from the bakery for his family to eat. Life was tough. Because of the money pressures Nathan faced, family life at the Silverstein house was tense.

Shel did not like school very much, and he was often bored in class. He doodled in the margins of his notebook during class

Even though formal education was never Shel's strong suit, he learned a great deal from his English teacher at Roosevelt University, Robert Cosbey.

time. Shel used drawing as an escape from boredom at school and tension at home.

Like many kids, Shel wished that he was better at different types of things. He said in an interview once, "When I was a kid—12, 14, around there—I would much rather have been a good baseball player or a hit with the girls. But I couldn't play ball, I couldn't dance. Luckily, the girls didn't want me; not much I could do about that. So, I started to draw and to write."

Shel's father, Nathan, did not appreciate Shel's drawing. He thought it was a useless distraction. Nathan wanted Shel to grow up to work in the family business. But Shel had other dreams.

Shel graduated from Roosevelt High School in 1948. After high school he attended the University of Illinois while he lived with his parents. Shel did not do very well. After the first year, he transferred to the Chicago Academy of Fine Arts, which is now called the Art Institute of Chicago. One of the courses of study at this school was cartooning, which seemed like the perfect fit for Shel.

His teachers at the Chicago Academy of Fine Arts wanted Shel to take their suggestions for how to improve his work. But Shel felt that he had produced his work just as he liked it the first time around. He did not want to change the drawings he did just because his teachers told him that he should. He only lasted about a year there, too.

Next, he went to school at Roosevelt University. It was affordable and convenient to Shel's home. There he met a teacher who would inspire him: Robert Cosbey. In fact, Shel's first children's book, *Lafcadio: The Lion Who Shot Back* was dedicated to Cosbey.

While Shel was at Roosevelt University, he worked on the student newspaper, called *The Roosevelt Torch*. Shel published his first cartoons in the newspaper. He also helped do layouts. Shel once said, "We were getting paid at the time too, but when I was there [the newspaper] had no money. There was a nice typewriter, though. It was a very old typewriter, so I accepted the typewriter in lieu of twenty-five dollars."

In 1953, Shel received a draft notice, which meant he had to leave school and serve in the military. Shel didn't mind too much. In fact, his military stint gave him his first professional creative work and gave him a taste for travel that he would pursue his whole life.

Shel's first trip was to Tokyo, Japan, in the 1950s during his time in the military. That trip inspired Shel to make travel a lifelong passion.

Chapter 2
STARS & STRIPES

"The Army was the best thing for me as far as my art work went because I didn't have to worry about coming through any commercial way.... I ate three meals a day, which is lucky because usually your meals depend on how well your stuff sells." (Stars & Stripes *interview*)

Shel sat on board a ship that was bringing him and his fellow troops to Japan for military service. The wild, wavy seas made Shel's stomach roil. Despite his seasickness, Shel drew cartoons. He and his friend, Bob Sweeney, worked on the ship's newspaper and started drawing cartoons to print in the paper.

Once Shel was stationed in Tokyo, he was placed in service of the Pacific version of the military newspaper *Stars & Stripes*. His job was to work on the layout of the paper and create photo features, which was similar to the work he did at Roosevelt University. In his spare time, Shel drew cartoons about military life. Soon, his cartoons started appearing in *Stars & Stripes*. After he had been working on the paper for several months, he convinced the editors

Even though Shel did not love some of the regulations of life in the military, he always remained grateful for the professional experience and the chance to publish his cartoons several times each week.

to allow him to travel around the region and report on various military experiences in the form of cartoons. Shel published about three cartoons per week. "For a guy of my age and with my limited experience to suddenly have to turn out cartoons on a day-to-day deadline, the job was enormous," Shel said of his writing for *Stars & Stripes* in a 1968 interview with the publication. "It was a great opportunity for me and I blossomed."

The military let him write about most things, but did not allow him to make jokes about the military itself. Shel tried to sneak in criticism about military life in his cartoons. Some of the cartoons were published and Shel got into trouble.

Military life could be difficult for Shel. He was a free spirit, so some of the rules of the military were hard for him to follow. But all throughout his life, Shel said that he appreciated the opportunities the military gave him. "It did me good, taught me things about life, and gave me freedom to create. The Army gave me an outlet for my work and it was great for me," Shel said in a *Stars & Stripes* interview.

In the Army, he began to travel widely. This was Shel's first experience traveling so far from home, and it planted a seed of wanderlust that would follow him his whole life. Shel had always tried to prove to his father that his drawings were worthwhile, and here he was, working as a cartoonist for the U.S. Army.

Shel did so many cartoons for the military that in 1955, two years after he began writing for *Stars & Stripes,* the Army published a book of his collected cartoons, called *Take Ten.* It was sold in military commissaries. In 1956, Ballantine Books published a reprint of *Take Ten* and called it *Grab Your Socks.* This book was sold as a paperback, available in bookstores all across the United States.

Shel was discharged from the military in the fall of 1955. His transition back to the relative freedom of home was not easy. He had a difficult time at first, but things would soon begin to turn around.

THE CATHOLICS IN AMERICA   THE REAL LITTLE ROCK STORY

LOOK

20¢ NOVEMBER 12, 1957

KIM NOVAK
A star
who wants to be
an actress

Sports Illustrated and Look
magazines were both important
publications in the United States
in the 1950s. Look magazine had
the second-highest circulation
of any magazine in the United
States at one point, second only
to Life magazine. Look folded—
or ceased publication—in 1971,
but Sports Illustrated is still
published to this day.

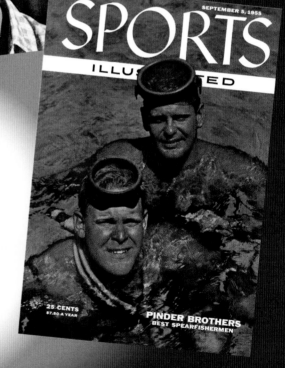

SEPTEMBER 5, 1955

SPORTS
ILLUSTRATED

25 CENTS
$7.50 A YEAR

PINDER BROTHERS
BEST SPEARFISHERMEN

Chapter 3
GAINING FAME

"In the beginning with an art form, you progress about 100 percent every day until you get good. Then, maybe you get to be 5 percent better each day."
(Stars & Stripes *interview*)

Coming back to the States without a job or a plan was difficult. His father's bakery had closed by the time Shel returned, so working in the family business was no longer an option. His father felt Shel should get a "real" job, something stable and full-time that did not have to do with silly drawings. But that was not Shel's style. He began to look for magazines that would publish his cartoons. He brought a portfolio of his work around to editors at magazines and hoped they would see something they liked.

Shel still lived with his parents and could not afford to move out. He desperately wanted to leave home and strike out on his own. At first he had trouble finding editors willing to publish his work. He was able to sell small cartoons to *Sports Illustrated* and *Look* magazines. But he was about to hit it big with a new men's magazine.

Chicago changed greatly over the course of Silverstein's life.

One day, Shel visited the offices of a magazine in his native Chicago that started as a new publication while Shel was overseas. He soon met with the magazine's publisher. Shel was not very impressed with the magazine at first. He left the offices after dropping off some samples, but he did not have very high hopes. The magazine's publisher was wearing pajamas when Shel met with him, which understandably seemed strange to Shel.

He thought the magazine might not even exist anymore when he returned a couple weeks later to get his portfolio back. But it did, and the publisher said he wanted to buy some of Shel's cartoons for his magazine. He bought about eight cartoons for around $600. A check was made out to Shel on the spot.

THE FAMILY LIFE OF A TRAVELING MAN

Although Shel never got married, he had two children. Shoshanna Hastings was born in 1970. Despite his amazing ability to relate to children through his written works, Shel struggled at first to relate to his own children. He always loved them very much, though. Shoshanna would spend a few weeks with Shel over summers and vacations. As she got older, Shoshanna gave Shel feedback about his children's poems and drawings. In 1982, Shoshanna died tragically and suddenly of a brain aneurysm. Shel was devastated.

In 1983, Shel had a son, named Matthew, with Sarah Spencer. Watching Matthew develop language as a young child inspired Shel to write a book of spoonerisms. A spoonerism is a language trick in which the first letters of two words are switched. Shel first mentioned to his editor his idea for a book of spoonerisms in the mid-1980s, but Runny Babbit was not published until more than twenty years later.

The very night he received his first payment, Shel moved out of his parents' house. He spent the next few months staying with friends in both Chicago and New York. New York was, and still is, the center of the publishing world in the United States. Shel wanted to be close to the action.

Shel missed traveling overseas, seeing exotic places, and meeting lots of different kinds of people. Luckily his new benefactor offered to publish cartoons about Shel's travels. So began a series of travelogues—written accounts of world destinations, accompanied by original cartoons. Shel traveled to and wrote about places such

SIXING MOUNDS

Spoonerisms are named for William Archibald Spooner (1844–1930), a priest in the Church of England. Spooner often accidentally mixed the initial sounds of words in his lectures and sermons. Some of his famous mix-ups include:

"The Lord is a shoving leopard"

"You have hissed all
        my mystery lectures"

"It is kisstomary to cuss the bride"

as London, Paris, Moscow, Africa, Mexico, and many others. From 1957 until 1968, Shel wrote twenty-three travelogues.

As Shel published more and more for different magazines, people began to notice his immense talent. A friend introduced Shel to an important children's book editor. She would help Shel become one of the most beloved and remembered children's authors of a generation. But first she had to convince Shel that it was a good idea.

All of Shel's travelogues have been collected into a book called *Silverstein Around the World*. It highlights Shel's experiences traveling in places like Moscow (top left), Africa (top right), Mexico (bottom left), and Paris (bottom right).

Shel's humor and wit tickle children and adults alike in his books of poems for children. Shel seems to relate to kids on a different level than most other grown-ups.

Chapter 4
CHILDREN'S BOOKS

In the early 1960s, Shel's friend Tomi Ungerer introduced him to Ursula Nordstrom, a children's editor for Harper & Row. Both Ungerer and Nordstrom thought Shel would be really good at writing for children. Shel, however, disagreed. He thought writing for children would be inappropriate for someone who made his living writing for a men's magazine. "I never planned to write or draw for kids," said Shel in a famous interview with the magazine *Publisher's Weekly*. "It was Tomi Ungerer, a friend of mine, who insisted . . . practically dragged me, kicking and screaming, into Ursula Nordstrom's office. And she convinced me that Tomi was right; I could do children's books."

Children's literature was once a way to show children how they should behave properly, with characters who dressed well and behaved perfectly, or showed the proper judgment in difficult situations. But Shel longed to appeal to children's more human nature, showing how children really think: how they can be silly, or on their worst behavior, or even sometimes sad. Shel believed children should be treated with respect and not spoken down to.

Shel also believed children wanted drawings that were detailed. "Children's illustrators are trying to draw like kids because they think kids will like it, but the last thing a kid wants to see is a drawing where he thinks he could have done it." Shel's illustrations were black-and-white line drawings that had a style that was uniquely his.

Shel's first book for children was *Lafcadio: The Lion Who Shot Back*, published in 1963. In the book, a marshmallow-loving lion named Lafcadio has a problem. After leaving his own habitat to go to the city and join the circus, he becomes too human to be considered a lion, but is still too much of a lion to be considered human. Shel always maintained that this was his favorite book he had written for children.

One of Shel Silverstein's most beloved books is *The Giving Tree*. It is also one of his more controversial books. In the story, a boy plays under a great apple tree, collecting her leaves, swinging from her branches, and eating her apples. As the boy grows, he asks for money and the tree offers him all of her apples so he can sell them for money. When the boy comes back as a man and says he wants a house, the tree lets him take all her branches and use the wood to build a house. When the boy is older still, he collects her trunk to build a boat. When he is an old man, he returns and uses her stump to rest. Through giving all of herself to the boy, the tree is happy. Some people said that the tree represented a mother giving everything she has to the boy until she has nothing left herself. Others hailed it as an example of selfless giving. Some people were angry that the boy never thanked the tree. Shel himself did not see the storyline as complicated as others seemed to interpret it. "It's just a relationship between two people; one gives and the other takes. I didn't start out to prove a message."

Shel published his books for adults with a different publisher, Simon & Schuster. Shel showed *The Giving Tree* to his editor there. Bob Cole, one of Shel's friends and an editor at Simon & Schuster, told him, "Look Shel, the trouble with this Giving Tree of yours is that it falls between two stools. It's not a kid's book – too sad – and it isn't for adults – too simple."

After it was rejected by Simon & Shuster, Shel showed *The Giving Tree* to Nordstrom and she eagerly accepted it. *The Giving Tree* had an initial print run of 7,000 copies. As of 2011, it had sold well over 8.5 million copies.

Although Shel wrote a number of books beginning in 1964, with a few published after his death in 1999, the following are just a few of his critically acclaimed titles.

Uncle Shelby's ABZ Book: Don't Bump the Glump and Other Fantasies (1961)

This book is a collection of cartoons and poems about fantastical made-up animals such as the Underslung Zath, the Bibely, the Long-Necked Preposterous, and the Gumplegutch. Although the book was intended by Shel to be for adults, many people assumed it was for children. In fact, HarperCollins Children's Books re-released the book in 2008, titling it *Don't Bump the Glump!: and Other Fantasies*.

A Giraffe and a Half (1964)

Published by Harper and Row, *A Giraffe and a Half* is a delightful book that uses rhymes to lead readers on a riotus tour of a giraffe that collects the most odd assortment of items, only to shed them all again by the end.

Who Wants a Cheap Rhinoceros? (1964)

In this Harper and Row title, Shel describes all the wonderful things having a rhinoceros could do for a person, such as helping collect allowance from Dad, playing jump rope, and using his horn to scratch your back.

Where the Sidewalk Ends (1974)

Originally titled *Uncle Shelby's Crazy Poems*, Shel worked on the poems and drawings of this book for more than a decade before its publication. Soon after *Where the Sidewalk Ends* was published, some school libraries banned the book. They worried that it would encourage children to misbehave because of poems like "How Not to Have to Dry the Dishes."

The Missing Piece (1976)

Published by Harper & Row, *The Missing Piece* is a single-story book that follows the journey of a circle-shaped creature that has a wedge-shaped piece missing from it. The creature rolls along searching for its missing piece, stopping along the way to sing, smell flowers, and chat with worms. Finally, after several failed tries, it

GENEROUS "AUTOGRAPHER"

Whenever people asked Shel to sign one of his children's books, he gave them the gift of a Shel Silverstein original drawing. The owner of a bookstore in Madison, Wisconsin said, "It was always a cartoon using the first letter of whoever's name he was autographing. To my knowledge, he would not just scribble out an autograph. It was a ten-minute operation."

meets its perfectly sized missing piece. Now it is complete and rolls along very fast since it is whole and perfectly round. But it realizes it cannot move slowly enough to smell flowers or chat with worms. Indeed it cannot even sing. So it gently puts the missing piece down and continues alone.

In 1981, a sequel to *The Missing Piece* was published, called *The Missing Piece Meets the Big O*. This book tells the same story, but from the piece's perspective.

A Light in the Attic (1981)

When Shel was writing his next collection of poems and illustrations, called *A Light in the Attic*, he sometimes needed feedback from children to help him work out the right words, or see what would be most appreciated by his audience. So Shel went to the nearest playground.

Shel was known for looking a little bit odd. He shaved his head and wore a full, bushy beard. He was known for wearing an old, worn leather jacket. So when he arrived at the playground to workshop some of his poems with kids, about half ran away from him, and half were curious about him and listened to his poems.

When *A Light in the Attic* was published in 1981, it spent 182 weeks on the *New York Times* bestseller list. Like *Where the Sidewalk Ends*, some people objected to some of the messages in the book. A school in Lake County, Florida, banned the book in the 1990s. But Shel ignored these critics and simply continued working on his craft.

It is clear from this impressive list of books Shel wrote for children that he had an abundance of creativity. But his creative genius was not limited to children's stories, poems, and illustrations.

SLOPPY SPELLER

Shel was known by his teachers in school and later his editors at HarperCollins for his terrible spelling. Once Shel was illustrating the cover of a program for a play he put on with Jean Shepherd in 1958 called "Look Charlie: A Short History of the Pratfall." On the cover, "Dorothy" is spelled wrong (Dorthy), as is "Charlie" (Chrlie). To fix the mistake in the word "Charlie," Shel drew in a few characters bringing in the letter 'd' to put in place.

THE FIVE-FINGERED HAND

One of Shel's inspirations was Virgil Partch, known as VIP. VIP was an illustrator for Walt Disney Studios. After he left Disney, VIP sometimes drew hands with dozens of fingers. In *American National Biography*, Partch explained, "At Disney's studio I spent four years drawing three fingers and a thumb. I'm just making up for that anatomical crime." With VIP as his inspiration, Shel always tried to draw a proper five-fingered hand in all of his illustrations.

As Shel got older, he traveled a little bit less often. He divided his time between a home in Key West, Florida, and a home in Martha's Vineyard, Massachusetts.

Chapter 5
A CREATIVE SOUL

Shel was not happy to work on just one type of creative project at a time. In addition to writing children's books and publishing cartoons and travelogues, Shel wrote music. One of his most famous songs is called "The Unicorn." A band called the Irish Rovers made it popular around 1967. The lyrics were a fable about unicorns being left behind by Noah's ark.

Another famous song written by Shel Silverstein is "A Boy Named Sue," which was made wildly popular when Johnny Cash sang it in 1969. It topped the *Billboard* country charts and hit number two on the pop charts. The next year, Shel won a Grammy for best country song for "A Boy Named Sue."

Shel loved to collaborate with other musicians to write songs. Usually other people performed the songs that Shel wrote, although he did release a few of his own albums. Shel worked a lot with Dr. Hook & The Medicine Show, Bobby Bare, Waylon Jennings, Kris Kristofferson, and many others. Shel even wrote scores for films. His song "I'm Checkin' Out," featured in the 1990 movie *Postcards from the Edge*, was nominated for an Oscar and a Golden Globe for

Johnny Cash first sang "A Boy Named Sue" at a concert he performed for San Quentin prison on February 24, 1969. Cash had heard the song just earlier that month at a party where Shel sang the song. Cash didn't have time to memorize the lyrics before the San Quentin performance, so he left the words on his music sheet and spoke many of the words.

best song in a motion picture. He was posthumously inducted into the Nashville Songwriters Hall of Fame in 2002.

Shel also won a Grammy for his album called *Where the Sidewalk Ends*, on which he reads poems from the book. Known for having a bit of a strange-sounding voice, his lively renditions of his poems help bring them to life in a very special way. Some of the poems are whispered in hushed tones, as though Shel is letting listeners in on a special secret. Others are brought to life with near-screaming and punctuated with well-timed moments of silence. His spoken poetry albums are available at libraries, and some samples can be heard online.

THE PLAYWRIGHT

Shel became known as a talented playwright. He wrote more than 100 one-act plays, some of which were performed at small theaters around New York and Chicago. Shel was a friend of the famed playwright David Mamet. All of Shel's plays were written for an adult audience.

BRINGING A CHILDREN'S BOOK TO LIFE: SHEL'S CREATIVE PROCESS

Shel's editors never knew exactly when Shel would deliver his next book. He had trouble keeping deadlines. Editors learned that Shel would almost certainly be late with his work. Ursula Nordstrom once wrote Shel a note that read: "You are a rotten nogoodnik to disappear for such long periods of time. Not even a postcard, you rat."

When an editor recommended a change to one of his poems, Shel could not simply change a word or two. No, Shel believed the poems had to spill out of his brain in one continuous writing session. "If I suggested that he change the poem in some way, even one word, and he agreed, he'd simply put it aside and come up with another version of it," said Joan Robins. "When he wrote, his words had to tumble all over the place or else it wasn't right for him."

Poetry collections took Shel a much longer time because he had to settle on the perfect order. The story *The Missing Piece*, for instance, was easier for Shel to lay out during the publishing process. The story had a natural beginning and end. With poetry collections, however, Shel went back and forth, changing the order in which the poems appeared, changing the placement of the art on the page, even by tiny increments, until he felt it was just right.

During this process, Shel worked in a conference room at his publisher's office. Nordstrom once said Shel's revisions involved "thousands of pieces of paper and millions of changes." Even when Shel thought it was finished, the layout usually changed several more times. When he worked on *A Light in the Attic*, the conference room work lasted for two months.

Once Shel had finalized artwork for his children's books, the drawings were printed and coated in a fine layer of wax. Then, Shel would put the waxed drawing on a large, slippery board so he could easily experiment with different placement of the art on the page.

Shel had a generous, collaborative spirit.
He worked on creative projects with many
neighbors and friends, often on his front porch.

Chapter 6
SHEL'S LEGACY

"The newness of something is what's exciting."
(*Stars & Stripes* interview)

Although Shel spent a lot of time with famous musicians, writers, and celebrities, many of whom lived a lifestyle of drugs and alcohol, Shel never did any drugs and very rarely drank any alcohol. Later in his life, he was known to practice Bikram yoga for three hours every morning. Coffee was his only vice. But Shel did not like to go to the doctor.

On May 9, 1999, Shel spoke on the phone to his lifelong friend Bobby Bare. Shel told Bobby he did not feel well and was going to bed early.

The next morning, his cleaning lady found him in his house. He had died of a heart attack in his home in Key West, Florida. He was 68 years old.

Shel never completed his book *Runny Babbit*, his book of spoonerisms, during his life, but he spent more than fifteen years working on it. In 2005, HarperCollins published *Runny Babbit*. It won a Quill Award in 2005 for best-illustrated children's book.

Mitch Myers, Shel's nephew, helps manage Shel's business now that he is gone. He works to make sure Shel's work continues to reach readers. Together with Shel's editors, Myers helped construct a book of children's poems that Shel had written, but did not have space to publish in his other books. The poems were collected into a book called *Every Thing On It*, which was published by HarperCollins in 2011. Some people wondered if the book would be as good as Shel's others since he was not there to oversee its layout and production. But Shel had already created some storyboards for a new collection, so his editors had some insight into what he envisioned for his next poetry collection.

Each of Shel's books continues to be sold as new readers discover his work. His memory will be brought to life with each new child who smiles at one of his poems, studies one of his detailed drawings, or laughs at a particularly clever spoonerism. It seems clear that Shel's work will stand the test of time, and he will continue to touch children's souls for many, many years to come.

SHEL'S BOOKS FOR CHILDREN

A Giraffe and a Half (HarperCollins, 1964)

A Light in the Attic (HarperCollins, 1981)

Uncle Shelby's Zoo: Don't Bump the Glump and Other Fantasies (HarperCollins, 1964)

Every Thing On It (HarperCollins, 2011)

Falling Up (HarperCollins, 1996)

The Giving Tree (HarperCollins, 1964)

Lafcadio: The Lion Who Shot Back (HarperCollins, 1963)

The Missing Piece (HarperCollins, 1976)

The Missing Piece Meets the Big O (HarperCollins, 1981)

Runny Babbit (HarperCollins, 2005)

Where the Sidewalk Ends (HarperCollins, 1974)

Who Wants a Cheap Rhinoceros? (Simon and Schuster, 1964)

GLOSSARY

commissary—a market for buying goods specifically for members of the military, often located on a military base

draft notice—a notification that says a person is required to enter into military service

layouts—the way words and images are set up on a printed page, such as a newspaper or a book

playwright—a person who writes plays

posthumously—meaning after death

score—a collection of music that is played during the action of a movie

spoonerism—mixing of the first sounds of two or more words, for example, instead of "yapping dog," a spoonerism is "dapping yog." Sometimes spoonerisms are intentional, but sometimes they occur by accident during normal speech

travelogue—a piece of writing that details a writer's travels to a destination

wanderlust—the desire to travel from place to place

CHRONOLOGY

September 25, 1930: Sheldon Allan Silverstein is born in Chicago, Illinois.

1935: Shel enters school and draws often, both at home and at school.

1944: Shel enters high school at Roosevelt High in Chicago and joins the ROTC, earning several honors, including a medal of General Excellence.

1951–53: Shel attends Roosevelt University and works on the *Roosevelt Torch*, doing paste-up and drawing cartoons.

September 1953: Shel is drafted into the U.S. Army.

1955: The Army publishes a collection of cartoons from *Stars & Stripes* called *Take Ten*. Shel is discharged from the Army.

1956: Ballantine Books publishes a version of *Take Ten* for civilians, calling it *Grab Your Socks*. It costs 35 cents.

August 1956: Shel's first cartoons are published in a popular men's magazine.

1960: *Now Here's My Plan*, Shel's first book of cartoons not about the military, is published.

1961: *Uncle Shelby's ABZ Book: A Primer for Young Minds* is published. Many people think this is a children's book, but Shel actually intended it for adults.

1962: Shel writes the song "The Unicorn," which is made famous by the Irish Rovers in 1967.

1963: Shel publishes his first children's book: *Lafcadio: The Lion Who Shot Back*.

1964: Shel publishes four books: *Uncle Shelby's Zoo: Don't Bump the Glump and Other Fantasies*, *A Giraffe and a Half*, *The Giving Tree*, and *Who Wants a Cheap Rhinoceros?*

1970: Shel's daughter, Shoshanna Hastings, is born. He wins a Grammy Award for his song "A Boy Named Sue."

1974: *Where the Sidewalk Ends* is published.

1975: Shel gives an interview to *Publisher's Weekly* magazine that becomes famous, partly because he gave so few interviews. Susan Hastings, the mother of his daughter, Shoshanna, dies. Shoshanna goes to live with her maternal grandparents.

1976: *The Missing Piece* is published.

1981: *A Light in the Attic* is published and goes on to spend 182 weeks on the *New York Times* bestseller list. *The Missing Piece Meets the Big O* is published. Shel's first play is produced.

1982: Shel's daughter, Shoshanna, dies unexpectedly at age eleven.

1983: Shel's son, Matthew, is born.

1991: Shel's song "I'm Checking Out" is nominated for an Oscar for best original song.

1996: *Falling Up* is published.

1998: *Draw a Skinny Elephant* is published.

1999: Shel dies of a heart attack in his home in Key West, Florida.

2005: *Runny Babbit*, Shel's book of spoonerisms, is published.

2011: *Every Thing On It* is published.

FURTHER INFORMATION

Books

Are you interested in trying to write stories yourself? These two books offer guidance.

Levine, Gail Carson. *Writing Magic: Creating Stories that Fly*. New York: Collins, 2006.

Messner, Kate. *Real Revision: Authors' Strategies to Share with Student Writers*. Portland, OR: Stenhouse, 2011.

Websites

Shel Silverstein official website: www.shelsilverstein.com.

Shel's page at the Academy of American Poets website: www.poets.org/poet.php/prmPID/104

The Poetry Foundation hosts special programs and resources to help children engage in poetry. www.poetryfoundation.org/children/

A collection of resources about reading and writing for kids of different ages. kids.usa.gov/reading-and-writing/index.shtml

BIBLIOGRAPHY

BOOKS

Rogak, Lisa. *A Boy Named Shel: The Life and Times of Shel Silverstein.* New York: St. Martin's Griffin. 2009.

ONLINE SOURCES

"All Time Best-Selling Children's Books." *Publisher's Weekly.* www. publishersweekly.com/pw/print/20011217/28595-all-time-bestselling-children-s-books.html.

Baldassaro, R. Wolf. "Banned Book Awareness: Shel Silverstein." Banned Book Awareness. August 15, 2011. bannedbooks.world. edu/2011/08/15/banned-books-awareness-shel-silverstein/.

Bird, Elizabeth. "Top 100 Picture Books." *School Library Journal.* July 6, 2012. blogs.slj.com/afuse8production/2012/07/06/top-100-picture-books-poll-results/.

Driscoll, Molly. "Shel Silverstein: A New Collection, 12 Years After His Death." *Christian Science Monitor*, September 21, 2011. www. csmonitor.com/Books/chapter-and-verse/2011/0921/Shel-Silverstein-a-new-collection-12-years-after-his-death.

Lodge, Sally. "A Look Behind Shel Silverstein's Bew Nook." *Publisher's Weekly*, February 28, 2005. www.publishersweekly.com/pw/print/20050228/17959-a-look-behind-shel-silverstein-s-bew-nook. html.

Lodge, Sally. "All-New Shel Silverstein Poetry Collection Due in 2011." *Publisher's Weekly*. March 18, 2010. www.publishersweekly.com/pw/by-topic/childrens/childrens-book-news/article/42487-all-new-shel-silverstein-poetry-collection-due-in-2011.html.

Mamet, David. "Theater: A Beloved Friend Who Lived Life the Chicago

Way." *New York Times*. October 14, 2001. www.nytimes.com/2001/10/14/
theater/theater-a-beloved-friend-who-lived-life-the-chicago-way.html.

Marshall, Elyse. "Shel Silverstein's First Poetry Collection - In Full
Color!" HarperCollins Press Release. November 2, 2011. www.
harpercollins.com/footer/release.aspx?id=613.

National Teacher's Association. "Teachers Top 100 Books for Children."
www.nea.org/grants/teachers-top-100-books-for-children.html.

NPR Staff. "Shel Silverstein's Poems Live On in 'Every Thing.'" *Morning
Edition*, September 20, 2011. Transcript: m.npr.org/story/140566486?a
mp;sc=tw&cc=share.

"Partch, Virgil Franklin II." *American National Biography Online*.
Oxford University Press. http://www.anb.org/articles/17/17-01692.
html.

"Shel Silverstein 1932-1999." *Publisher's Weekly*, May 17, 1999.
www.publishersweekly.com/pw/print/19990517/19696-shel-
silverstein-1932-1999.html.

"Shel Silverstein Stars & Stripes Interview, 1968." From *Off On a
Tangent*, used with permission of *Stars & Stripes*. offonatangent.
tumblr.com/post/9279976269/shel-silverstein-stars-stripes-
interview-1968.

Paul, Pamela. "The Children's Authors Who Broke The Rules." *New York
Times*, September 16, 2011. www.nytimes.com/2011/09/18/books/
review/the-childrens-authors-who-broke-the-rules.html?_r=1&.

Weinman, Sarah. "Shel Silverstein Comes Alive in a New Book,
Published 12 Years After his Death." *The Atlantic*. September 20, 2011.
www.theatlantic.com/entertainment/archive/2011/09/shel-silverstein-
comes-alive-in-a-new-book-12-years-after-his-death/245228/.

Weinman, Sarah. "The Shel Silverstein Archive." November 14, 2003. www.webring.org/l/rd?ring=shelsilversteinw;id=2;url=http%3A%2F%2Fshelsilverstein.tripod.com%2F.

INDEX

ABOUT THE AUTHOR:

Johannah Haney is a freelance writer and a professor living in Boston. She has written more than a dozen nonfiction books for young readers, as well as articles and essays in national magazines. Johannah teaches publishing and writing at Emerson College. She fondly remembers reading Shel Silverstein poems growing up.